Why Organizations Should Develop Their Leaders: Pocket Guide

Sections:

Introduction:

Leadership is a critical component of organizational success, and effective leadership development programs are essential for growing and retaining talented leaders. *Why Organizations Should Develop Their Leaders: Pocket Guide* provides a quick but comprehensive guide to leadership development, drawing on best practices and real-world examples from my military service to help readers create and implement successful programs.

Look, after I retired from the military and held a couple of civilian jobs, I learned that many businesses do not intentionally develop their managers. This guide is designed for professionals and organizations looking to enhance their leadership development strategies. It covers a wide range of topics, from understanding leadership styles and behaviors to fostering innovation and managing change. The sections in this guide provide practical advice and actionable steps for readers to apply to their own leadership development programs. This is not an all-inclusive solution. In order to implement a leadership development program, you either need to consult someone who has a comprehensive understanding and knowledge of leadership development programming or hire a leadership coach or consultant. Throwing crap at the wall and seeing what sticks is not a solution for poor management.

This guide is organized into fourteen sections. The first section provides an overview of leadership development and introduces the key concepts and strategies that will be covered throughout the guide. The subsequent sections delve into specific areas of leadership development, including communication, emotional intelligence, critical thinking, and team building. The final section explores emerging trends and best practices in leadership development, offering insights from an old Soldier about what works and what doesn't.

Bottom Line Up Front (BLUF), the military invests a significant amount of time into developing their leaders because we NEED, not wan,t but NEED to be able to rely on one another and trust the decision-making skills of the leaders appointed over us. What I am about to share with you, however brief it may be, are the best practices of what it takes to fight and win, no matter what type of organization you have. Developing your leaders is absolutely essential to the success of your organization.

1: What is Leadership Development?

According to FM 6-22 (US Army Field Manual)

Leadership:
> Providing purpose, direction, and motivation while operating to accomplish the mission and improve the organization.

Leadership Development:
> The process of enhancing the skills, abilities, and behaviors of individuals to help them become effective leaders.

Leadership development involves a range of activities, from training and coaching to mentoring and job assignments. The goal of leadership development is to create a pipeline of talented leaders who can drive organizational success.

There are several key components of effective leadership development programs.

- The program needs to be aligned with the organization's overall strategy and goals. This ensures that the development of leaders is integrated into the broader organizational context and supports the organization's mission.

- Effective leadership development programs are based on a clear understanding of the competencies and behaviors that are critical for success in leadership roles. These competencies may include communication, emotional intelligence, critical thinking, and decision-making, among others. Another component that will be discussed will be the importance of decentralizing your organization.

- Leadership development programs should be tailored to the specific needs of individual leaders and the organization as a whole. This may involve counseling, coaching, and job assignments that provide opportunities for growth and development.

- Effective leadership development programs should be evaluated regularly to measure their impact and identify areas for improvement. This may involve surveys, interviews, and other data collection methods to assess the effectiveness of the program.

- Setting and managing expectations, combined with getting to know your employee's strengths and weaknesses, is also vital. This provides a feedback and communications system while making sure your people are placed in the best possible position.

In the subsequent sections of this guide, we will explore each of these components in more detail, providing practical guidance and examples to help organizations create and implement effective leadership development programs.

2: Understanding Leadership Styles and Behaviors

Leadership styles and behaviors play a critical role in determining the success of leaders and their organizations. Effective leaders understand their own style and adapt it to the situation and the needs of their team. This section will explore different leadership styles and behaviors and how they impact organizational outcomes.

There are several different leadership styles, including, but not limited to:

- Transformational

    Inspire and motivate their teams to achieve their goals

- Transactional

    Uses rewards and punishments to influence behavior

- Servant leadership

    Prioritize the needs of their team and focus on helping the members of the team grow and develop

I am a firm believer that if you are a servant leader, you will automatically or by extension, create transformational leadership.

Every company uses a combination of all three of these leadership styles. There have to be standards and discipline from transactional leaders, or chaos ensues; however, if a professional environment is too relaxed, then there is no direction. There must be an equalizing balance and blend of all three styles. With this in mind, disciplinary action should be secondary to teaching, coaching, and mentoring.

In addition to leadership styles, there are also different leadership behaviors that impact organizational outcomes. These behaviors include:

- Communication

Effective leaders communicate clearly and listen actively to their team

- Decision-making

    Make informed decisions based on data and input from others

- Conflict resolution

    Resolve conflicts in a constructive and collaborative manner

Understanding leadership styles and behaviors is critical for effective leadership development. By providing leaders with the tools and knowledge to adapt their style and behaviors to the situation, organizations can improve their leadership capacity and achieve their goals.

In the subsequent sections of this guide, we will explore strategies for developing leadership styles and behaviors, providing practical guidance and examples to help organizations create and implement effective leadership development programs.

3: Developing Leadership Competencies

Leadership Competencies:

The skills, knowledge, and abilities that effective leaders possess.

Developing these competencies is essential for leaders to be successful in their roles and to drive organizational growth and success. In this section, we will discuss key leadership competencies and strategies for developing them.

Some of the key leadership competencies include:

- Strategic Thinking

  Strategic thinking is the ability to use analytical and critical thinking skills to create and communicate a clear vision and develop plans to achieve that vision.

- Emotional Intelligence

  The ability to recognize and manage one's own emotions in order to maintain good order and discipline and always make clear, impartial decisions.

- Problem-Solving

  These skills are essential for leaders to identify and successfully address challenges that arise in the workplace.

- Team Building

  Creating a positive and inclusive work environment where team members feel valued and motivated to work towards shared goals.

To develop leadership competencies, organizations can provide a range of training and development opportunities, including mentorship, coaching, quarterly leadership training, and workshops. Additionally, organizations can create leadership development programs that focus on building specific competencies, such as emotional intelligence or team building.

Effective leadership development programs should be tailored to the needs of individual leaders and the organization as a whole. They should be designed to address specific gaps in leadership competencies and provide opportunities for leaders to practice and apply new skills in the workplace. By investing in leadership development, organizations can build a strong leadership pipeline and ensure the long-term success of their organization.

In the following sections, we will briefly dive deeper into strategies for developing specific leadership competencies, providing practical guidance and real-world examples to help organizations build effective leadership development programs.

4: Building a Strong Leadership Culture
A strong leadership culture is essential for the success of any organization. It ensures that leaders at all levels of the organization are aligned with the company's mission and values and are able to inspire and motivate their teams to achieve their goals. In this section, we will discuss strategies for building a strong leadership culture.

As a side note, it needs to be said that strong leaders get to know their teams. If you want to incorporate any sort of strategy, you must understand the strengths and weaknesses of everyone on your team.

3 Key Strategies for Building a Strong Leadership Culture:

1. Ensure that leadership development is a top priority for the organization.

    a. Invest in training and development programs for leaders at all levels of the organization and provide opportunities for them to develop their skills and competencies.

    b. Create a culture that supports and encourages leadership development, with leaders at all levels serving as role models and mentors for others. If you don't invest in an organization to do this for you, you should ensure that you develop people within the organization at every level that will be able to provide this training and development.

2. Establish clear expectations and standards for leadership within the organization.

    a. Define the competencies and behaviors that are required of leaders at each level of the organization and hold them accountable for meeting those expectations.

b. Create a culture of feedback and continuous improvement where leaders are provided with regular feedback on their performance and are encouraged to seek out opportunities for growth and development. The military has monthly counseling sessions for execution-level employees and quarterly counseling sessions for people in leadership positions with an annual review. This may not be right for your organization, but it is an example to follow.

3. Creating a strong leadership culture also involves fostering a sense of shared purpose and commitment to the organization's mission and values.

a. Communicate the organization's mission and values clearly and consistently and ensuring that all leaders and employees understand how their work contributes to achieving the organization's goals.

b. Opportunities must also be created for collaboration and teamwork and should be recognized and rewarded for those who demonstrate strong leadership skills and behaviors.

I served in the Army and though every organization had a different mission, there was a set of values that flowed through the entire military branch. It actually had the acronym LDRSHIP; Loyalty, Duty, Respect, Selfless Service, Honor, Integrity, and Personal Courage. I have actually found that not many organizations outside of the military have even taken the time to establish a company mission or a set of values. This is important and should be done for EVERY organization.

In the next section, we will explore the role of leadership communication in building a strong leadership culture and provide practical guidance for leaders on how to clearly communicate their vision, values, and expectations to their teams.

5: The Role of Communication in Building a Strong Leadership Culture

Effective communication is a critical component of strong leadership and is essential for building a strong leadership culture. In this section, we will explore the role of communication in building a strong culture and provide practical guidance for leaders on how to effectively communicate their vision, values, and expectations to their teams.

Communication involves more than just conveying information.

It involves:

- Creating a sense of shared purpose and commitment among team members

- Inspiring and motivating team members to work towards common goals

- Building trust and credibility

To be effective, leaders must be able to communicate in a way that resonates with their audience and is tailored to the needs and preferences of different team members.

3 Key Strategies for Building a Strong Culture

1. Be clear and concise in your messaging.

    a. Communicate your vision, values, and expectations in a way that all team members easily understand.

    b. Use language that is appropriate for your audience, avoiding jargon or technical language that may be unfamiliar to some team members.

2. Be authentic in your communication.

    a. Communicate in a way that is consistent with your personality and style, and that reflects your genuine beliefs and values. Authentic communication builds trust and credibility and helps to create a sense of connection and shared purpose among team members.

3. Effective leadership communication also involves active listening and feedback.

   a. Take the time to listen to your team members' concerns and ideas and provide feedback and guidance to help them improve their performance.

   b. Create opportunities for team members to provide feedback to you and be open and receptive to their suggestions and ideas.

In the next section, we will explore the role of coaching and mentorship in leadership development and provide practical guidance for leaders on how to coach and mentor their team members to build a strong leadership culture.

6: Coaching and Mentorship in Leadership Development

Coaching and mentorship are essential components of leadership development and are important for building a strong leadership culture. In this section, we will explore the role of coaching and mentorship in leadership development and provide practical guidance for leaders on how to coach and mentor their team members effectively.

Coaching

Coaching is providing guidance, feedback, and support to team members to help them improve their skills and performance. Think of this as teaching someone to fish rather than giving them a fish. Effective coaching involves active listening, asking open-ended questions, and providing constructive feedback. It also involves setting clear goals and expectations and providing regular check-ins to monitor progress and provide additional support as needed.

Mentorship

Mentorship, on the other hand, is being involved in a team member's professional development but sitting back and providing additional guidance and support on an "as needed" basis. Effective mentorship involves building a strong relationship of trust and respect with your mentee, providing constructive feedback and guidance, and sharing your own experiences and insights to help them grow and develop.

To be an effective coach or mentor, it is important to have strong interpersonal skills.

Interpersonal Skills to Develop:

- Active listening

- Empathy

- The ability to build trust and rapport with others

- Having a clear understanding of your mentee's strengths, weaknesses, and goals

- Tailoring your coaching and mentoring approach to the individual needs and preferences of the mentee

Effective coaching and mentorship can help to build a strong leadership culture by empowering team members to take ownership of their own development and by creating a culture of continuous learning and improvement. By providing guidance and support to team members, leaders can help them to develop the skills and competencies needed to become effective leaders themselves and contribute to the overall success of the organization. In the next section, we will explore Emotional Intelligence in Leadership.

7: Emotional Intelligence in Leadership

Emotional intelligence is a critical component of effective leadership. In this section, we will explore the importance of emotional intelligence in leadership and provide practical guidance for leaders on how to develop their emotional intelligence skills to become more effective leaders.

Emotional Intelligence:

The ability to recognize and manage one's own emotions in order to maintain good order and discipline and always make clear, impartial decisions. It involves a range of skills, including:

- Self-awareness

    Be honest with oneself about one's strengths and weaknesses, as well as one's emotional triggers and reactions.

- Self-regulation

    Managing stress in a healthy way and avoiding emotional outbursts.

- Empathy

    Understand and appreciate the perspectives and feelings of others. Leaders can develop empathy by actively listening to team members and by seeking to understand their concerns and viewpoints.

- Social skills

    The ability to communicate effectively, build strong relationships, and work collaboratively with others. Leaders can develop their social skills by practicing effective communication, building strong relationships with team members, and seeking out opportunities for collaboration and teamwork.

Effective leaders with strong emotional intelligence are better able to manage their own emotions, which allows them to remain calm and focused in high-pressure situations. They are also able to read and respond to the emotions of others, which allows them to build strong relationships with team members and stakeholders. Let me be clear on something, leaders that cannot manage their emotions are going to be alone on an island because no one, senior, peer, or subordinate, will want to deal with an emotional roller-coaster.

By developing their emotional intelligence skills, leaders can become more effective in managing their own emotions, building strong relationships with team members and stakeholders, and creating a positive and productive work environment. In the next section, we will explore the importance of ownership as a leader and how it creates and builds relationships.

8: Ownership as a Leader and How it Creates and Builds Relationships

The idea of ownership can be very confusing to some people.

Ownership:

Simply put, ownership is taking all responsibility for everything that happens in your sphere of influence. When I say everything, I mean everything! Here are some key considerations when thinking about ownership and how it can build trust and confidence within the workforce:

1. The first thing to consider is that ownership is a choice.

   What this means is that every leader within an organization must choose if they want to accept the ultimate responsibility of any outcome within their team and/or sphere of influence. This is not something that comes naturally. It needs to be trained and pointed out as a specific quality that is needed if people wish to serve as a leader within an organization.

2. Next, when taking ownership, a leader needs to be decisive, emphatic, and absolute in their decision-making.

   This means that they are making decisions clearly with the understanding that they are willing to accept all consequences, positive or negative, that may result from that decision.

3. Regular objective reflection is an essential aspect of taking ownership.

   As a leader, you need to reflect on events and their outcomes regularly. You must analyze what went well and what didn't go well. Identify areas for improvement and take action to make changes. When you reflect on events objectively, you show your team that you are committed to continuous improvement.

4. Here is the most important part, leaders must take ownership of all the things that their team members do, right and wrong.

> Leaders should never place the blame on their subordinates. When a member of a team does something wrong, so often, the first thing that most leaders think is, "How was I supposed to be able to control their actions/decisions?" The answer to this question is simple (but it is a hard pill to swallow). All consequences (positive or negative) that occur on your team are YOUR RESPONSIBILITY...OWN IT!! You should KNOW your team and mitigate as many risks as possible. If you know the members of your team, you should know who to trust and who not to trust. How much or how little instruction to give someone before sending them off to do a task.

The reason why ownership is important is that you want your seniors, peers, and subordinates to trust you. If you are flaky and you never take responsibility for your actions, most employers will not trust you to do anything. Make decisions, own those decisions, lead people, and own all the work they do. If you do these things, you will not just be looked on as an authority; you will become the authority.

The concept of ownership is easy, but again, it is not easy to execute. Make sure this is part of your leadership development program because leaders need to be taught what this is, what it means, and why it is important. In the next section, we will discuss the importance of ethical leadership and provide practical guidance for leaders on how to foster a culture of integrity and ethical behavior within their organizations.

9: Ethical Leadership

There have been many high-profile examples of unethical behavior in business, from financial scandals to workplace harassment. As a result, there has been a growing recognition of the importance of ethical leadership in organizations. Ethical leaders not only model ethical behavior themselves but also create a culture of integrity and ethical decision-making within their organizations.

At its core, **Ethical Leadership** involves:

- Making decisions that are guided by moral principles and values, and that are in the best interests of all stakeholders, not just shareholders.

- Being transparent and honest in communications, treating employees with respect and dignity, and holding oneself and others accountable for ethical behavior.

To build a culture of ethical leadership within their organizations, leaders can do the following:

- Start by establishing a code of ethics or a set of values that guide decision-making and behavior. This code should be communicated clearly and consistently to all employees and reinforced through training and regular reminders.

- Model ethical behavior themselves by being transparent and open in their communications, treating employees with respect and fairness, and making decisions that are guided by ethical principles rather than personal gain. They should also be willing to acknowledge and rectify mistakes and unethical behavior and hold themselves and others accountable for ethical lapses.

Another key aspect of ethical leadership is creating a culture of ethical decision-making within the organization.
This Includes:

- Empower employees to speak up and report ethical concerns without fear of retaliation and provide them with the support and resources they need to do so.

- Ensuring that all decisions are made with consideration for their impact on stakeholders, including employees, customers, and the broader community.

By building a culture of ethical leadership, leaders can create an environment that is not only more resilient and adaptable but also more trustworthy and respected by stakeholders. In the next section, we will explore the importance of resilience in leadership and provide practical guidance for leaders on how to build resilience within themselves and their teams.

10: Resilient Leadership
Resilience:

The ability to adapt to and recover from adversity. Resilience is a critical skill for leaders to have in today's rapidly changing business landscape. Resilient leaders can stay calm under pressure, bounce back from setbacks, and inspire their teams to do the same. In this section, we will explore the importance of resilient leadership and provide practical guidance for leaders on how to build resilience within themselves and their teams.

Resilient leadership:

- Recognizing that setbacks and challenges are a natural part of the business world and being prepared to handle them when they arise.

- Developing a mindset of growth and learning and viewing failures and setbacks as opportunities for growth and development.

- Being proactive about identifying potential risks and challenges and developing contingency plans to address them.

To build resilience within themselves, leaders can start by practicing self-care and stress management techniques.
This can include:

- Regular exercise

- Meditation

- Mindfulness practices

- Taking time to disconnect from work and recharge.

- Seeking out support from mentors, coaches, or other trusted advisors, who can provide guidance and perspective during challenging times.

Leaders can also build resilience within their teams by fostering a culture of psychological safety and support. This means creating an environment where team members feel comfortable sharing their thoughts and concerns and where feedback is encouraged and valued. It also means providing opportunities for professional development and growth and recognizing and rewarding team members for their contributions. Another key aspect of resilient leadership is being able to effectively manage change. This means being adaptable and flexible, and willing to pivot when needed. It also means communicating clearly, transparently and consistently with team members about changes and how they will be impacted while providing the necessary support and resources to help them navigate through transitions.

By building resilience within themselves and their teams, leaders can create a culture of strength and adaptability that is better equipped to handle challenges and thrive in the face of adversity. In the next section, we will discuss why innovation is an important quality to have included in your leadership development program.

11: Innovative Leadership

Innovation is critical for organizational success in today's fast-paced and constantly evolving business landscape. Leaders who can foster a culture of innovation within their organizations are better equipped to respond to changing market conditions, identify new opportunities, and stay ahead of the competition. In this section, we will explore the importance of innovative leadership and provide practical guidance for leaders on how to foster a culture of innovation within their organizations.

Innovative leadership:

Creating an environment that encourages and supports creativity and experimentation:

- Provide the resources and support necessary for employees to take risks, try new approaches, and challenge the status quo.

- Foster a culture of continuous learning and improvement where feedback is encouraged, and mistakes are viewed as opportunities for growth and development.

Steps to Creating a Culture of Innovation

1. Establishing a clear vision and strategy for innovation within the organization.
    a. Include specific goals and objectives, as well as a plan for how innovation will be integrated into the organization's overall strategy.
    b. Leaders should also communicate the importance of innovation to all team members and create a sense of urgency and excitement around the pursuit of new ideas and approaches.
2. Empowering employees to take ownership of the innovation process.
    a. Give employees the autonomy and freedom to explore new ideas, take risks, and make decisions.

  b. Provide the necessary resources and support, such as time, funding, and access to technology, to help employees bring their ideas to life.
3. Creating a diverse and inclusive workplace culture.
  a. Value and respect diverse perspectives and experiences and actively seek out input and feedback from a range of sources.
  b. Provide opportunities for underrepresented groups to participate in the innovation process and ensure that everyone has an equal chance to contribute to the organization's success.

By fostering a culture of innovation, leaders can create a dynamic and adaptable organization that is better equipped to respond to changing market conditions and stay ahead of the competition. In the next section, we will explore the importance of decentralized leadership and provide practical guidance for leaders on how to develop and execute effective strategies for their organizations.

12: Decentralized Leadership

Decentralized Leadership:

A leadership model in which decision-making power is distributed throughout an organization rather than being concentrated at the top.

In a decentralized organization, leaders at all levels are empowered to make decisions and take action, rather than waiting for direction from above. This model of leadership is characterized by the dispersion of authority for decision-making at all levels of leadership within the organization.

Decentralized leadership has become increasingly popular in recent years as organizations seek to become more agile, responsive, and innovative. Here are some reasons why decentralized leadership matters:

- Flexibility:

    Decentralized leadership allows organizations to be more flexible and adaptable to changing circumstances. Leaders at all levels are empowered to make decisions and take action, which allows the organization to respond quickly to new challenges and opportunities.

- Creativity:

    Decentralized leadership encourages creativity and innovation by empowering leaders at all levels to come up with new ideas and solutions. This can lead to breakthroughs and competitive advantages that would not be possible in a more centralized organization.

- Empowerment:

    Decentralized leadership empowers leaders at all levels to take ownership of their work and make decisions that impact the organization. This can lead to greater job satisfaction and engagement among employees.

- Future-ready:

Decentralized leadership is well-suited to the future of work, which is characterized by remote work, distributed teams, and rapid change. Decentralized organizations are better equipped to navigate these challenges and thrive in the new normal.

Implementing decentralized leadership requires a shift in mindset and culture. Here are some steps organizations can take to implement decentralized leadership:

- Empower leaders at all levels:

    Leaders at all levels should be empowered to make decisions and take action. This requires trust and a willingness to let go of control.

- Encourage collaboration:

    Decentralized leadership requires collaboration and communication across teams and departments. Leaders should encourage collaboration and provide the tools and resources needed to facilitate it.

- Provide training and support:

    Leaders at all levels may need training and support to develop the skills needed to make decisions and take action. Organizations should provide the training and support needed to help leaders succeed.

Measure and adjust: Decentralized leadership require ongoing measurement and adjustment. Organizations should measure the impact of decentralized leadership and adjust their approach as needed to ensure success.

Decentralized leadership is a powerful model of leadership that can help organizations become more agile, responsive, and innovative. By empowering leaders at all levels to make decisions and take action, organizations can thrive in the new normal and achieve their goals. To implement decentralized leadership, organizations must be willing to let go of control, encourage collaboration, provide training and support, and measure and adjust their approach as needed. In the next section, I will be talking about the development of the leadership program itself.

13: Creating a Leadership Development Program

In order to build a strong pipeline of future leaders, organizations need to invest in a comprehensive leadership development program. Such a program should be designed to identify and develop high-potential employees and to provide them with the skills and experiences they need to succeed in leadership roles.

Steps to Create a Leadership Development Program:

1. Assess the organization's current leadership capabilities and identify areas where improvement is needed. This may involve conducting a leadership assessment, gathering feedback from employees and stakeholders, and benchmarking against industry best practices.

2. Once the organization has a clear understanding of its leadership needs and gaps, it can begin to design a program that meets those needs. This may involve a range of activities, such as leadership training, mentoring, coaching, job rotations, and stretch assignments.

3. Each company's program should be tailored to the specific needs of its organization and should be aligned with its strategic goals and objectives. The program should also be flexible enough to adapt to changing business needs and to the evolving needs of individual leaders.

4. Programs should also be designed to foster a culture of continuous learning and growth. This means encouraging all employees to take ownership of their own development and providing them with the tools and resources they need to build their skills and capabilities.

5. Leadership development programs should be evaluated on a regular basis to ensure that they

meet the needs of the organization and deliver the desired results. This may involve collecting feedback from participants, measuring the impact of development activities, and adjusting as needed to ensure continuous improvement.

By investing in a comprehensive leadership development program, organizations can build a strong pipeline of future leaders and position themselves for long-term success in an ever-changing business environment.

14: Overcoming Leadership Challenges

Even the most effective leaders face challenges and obstacles on their journey to success. In this section, we will explore some common leadership challenges and strategies for overcoming them.

1. Dealing with change:

    In today's fast-paced business environment, change is inevitable. As a leader, it's important to be able to adapt to change and to help your team navigate it as well.

    a. Communicate clearly and frequently with your team about changes and the implications of those changes.

    b. Build resilience and agility by encouraging a growth mindset and providing opportunities for learning and development.

2. Managing conflict:

    Conflict is a natural part of any workplace, and as a leader, it's your job to manage it effectively.

    a. Focus on the underlying interests and needs of all parties involved and work together to find a solution that meets everyone's needs.

    b. Foster a culture of open communication and mutual respect and model constructive conflict resolution behaviors.

3. Building trust:

    Trust is essential for effective leadership, but it takes time and effort to build.

    a. Be transparent and authentic in your communications and actions.

b. Demonstrate your trustworthiness by keeping your commitments, being accountable for your actions, and showing empathy and support for your team.

4. Motivating and engaging employees:

Keeping your team motivated and engaged is critical for achieving success.

a. Understand what drives and motivates each team member and provide opportunities for growth and development.

b. Create a positive work environment by recognizing and celebrating achievements, fostering a sense of purpose and meaning, and promoting work-life balance.

5. Making tough decisions:

As a leader, you will inevitably face difficult decisions that have a significant impact on your organization and team.

a. Make decisions effectively, it's important to gather and analyze all relevant information, seek input from key stakeholders, and consider the potential consequences of each option.

b. It's important to communicate your decision clearly and transparently, and to provide support and guidance to your team as they navigate any resulting changes.

By understanding and proactively addressing these common leadership challenges, you can become a more effective and successful leader and help your organization achieve its goals and objectives.

Conclusion:

Leadership development is a journey that requires commitment, self-awareness, and continuous learning. In this guide, we've explored the foundations of leadership, the importance of emotional intelligence, strategies for building effective teams, and common leadership challenges and how to overcome them. Whether you're a new leader just starting out or an experienced leader looking to enhance your skills, there's always room for growth and improvement.

To become a great leader, it's important to focus on your strengths, identify areas for improvement, and seek out opportunities for learning and development. This might include seeking out a mentor or coach, attending leadership development programs, or reading books and articles on leadership.

As you continue your leadership journey, remember that leadership is not just about achieving results but also about inspiring and empowering others to achieve their full potential. By cultivating a culture of trust, transparency, and collaboration, you can create a work environment where everyone can thrive and contribute to the success of your organization.

Thank you for reading this guide on leadership development. I hope that it has provided you with valuable insights and strategies for becoming a more effective leader. Remember, leadership is a journey, not a destination, and the best leaders are always seeking ways to learn, grow, and improve.